Gatekeepers:
Guardians of a Community

JoeAnn Ballard

Optimum Publishing

A division of Optimum Studios

735 N. Parkway

Memphis, TN 38105

Special thanks to

Sharon Lucas Taylor for her contribution.

Table of Contents

Dedicated to Doris Alexander - my 4th grade teacher

Thank you Mrs. Alexander for teaching me to love my community.

Introduction

The American Family, for most of our history, has been a community of people who believed in accommodating each other's needs. It was a community within a larger community, which was characterized as respectful, sharing, caring, and loving. It consisted of a likeminded people focused on personal and community growth. One's dreams, goals, and visions, for his family and the wider community, were to develop a better environment in which to live so that everyone was empowered. The American Family's standards of living, at the time, were motivated by a patriarchal ideology; the men cultivated the land, an important part of their culture, and were the head of the household.

Families were known to work long, hard days, and their children followed in their parents' footsteps. Moreover, the families in the communities owned their land, their homes, and their livestock: all of which contributed to a family's social status. Another important social component was education, which was so important that it gained a community focus. Families ensured their children were afforded this. Although parents paid special attention to education, they did not escape the difficulties of the period. There were no school buses, so children had to walk two or three miles to school each day. Parents ensured their children attended schools closest to their homes. The family system followed a process of order that sustained their lives.

Families demonstrated a level of interdependence amongst one another. Notwithstanding, families maintained their independence unless some personal decisions needed assistance from the community. Other families, especially older members, were consulted on matters that were deemed too difficult to solve alone. Families practiced a civilized lifestyle, which increased relationships, a sense of autonomy was expressed, and solidarity was practiced. Families were common, ordinary people building, growing, and making their future plans count. Therefore, families in the 1800s lived and worked to expand their communities. Despite all odds, they invested in helping each other.

The African American Family after the Emancipation Proclamation

The African American Family, also known as the Black Family, was a hidden community that existed simultaneously as a unique community and within the broader community. Some challenges, such as slavery, made an impact on the social relationships within of their community; it divided the Black Family, but it did not completely sever family ties. They created makeshift villages in which to live, and some families were united while others were not.

The legacy of slavery provided serious economic maladies for the Black Family. Their poor economic situation was a prevailing factor that hindered them, along with the displacement of family members, which suppressed them even more. In order to move forward, they worked together to strengthen their village. So, in spite of their losses, they remained a strong family unit, making them a cohesive community.

As a family unit, they faced many obstacles, but they endured and approached life differently. When they could no longer find their family members, they created a "kinship network" by claiming unrelated people as family. During this era, African Americans placed high priority the family unit, kin, and community.

The father's role within this family unit was important; however, there was a matriarchal influence that remained stronger. Sometimes it was a distant relationship between father and family, especially since he had to maintain their economic stability and work several miles from home. After slavery, they became wage laborers or sharecroppers. So to sustain familial ties, the women worked on the farm and in the home. They adapted to difficult circumstances, while continuing

8

to nurture the children who were stressing and participating in their education. To maintain family stability, children helped in the fields, attended school, and helped with the chores. Despite many cultural distractions, African American families remained focused on church, family roots, human worth, and stability.

The Changing Family

Generally, the original village consisted of a mixed family. Most families had both parents- mama and papa. Some families quickly beat the odds and became self-sufficient, while there were some that relied on others. Some were educated and some were not. Single mothers relied on their parents to raise their children so that they could continue their education while working and, widows relied on assistance from in-laws and close relatives. Some men assumed the role as gatekeepers in the village. The village remained strong because it was made up of all these people. Therefore, an extended family replaced the shock of a fragmented family.

The extended family had key roles in supporting the nuclear families, and the entire village depended upon this fact during hard times. In fact, the entire village became almost an extended family, facilitating order in difficult circumstances. If someone got laid off as a seasonal worker, they created a job for that individual. Because the village had a gatekeeper, they were assured of some help, which sustained them. Whatever the families needed, the extended family created ways of preserving the village- hog killing. Gatekeepers were those men who gauged the health of the community and were able to provide, organize, and direct others to help or assist within the community. They had no official position; however, they were treated as though they all had authority.

Families in the village shared food, and if a neighbor needed sugar, the villages provided it; if a neighbor needed vegetables, they could go to the garden and get some. They could walk through the village and smell dairy products, meat, and greens cooking. Mothers were sweeping off sidewalks, flowers were growing in the garden, and babies were being born. Because of the gatekeepers, the village was a safe place to live.

11

The village was strong and self-sufficient. They lived as an enormous family with deep roots that were embedded in rich soil. In the village, most families embodied the same family values. The true village found ways to be involved with similar social demands in life: they were committed to the same churches, same schools, and same grocery stores. The gatekeepers functioned almost as non-elected mayors and helped the entire village with its needs. They might create a schedule that allowed trips to grocery stores, which helped the women; they appointed a laborer to transport them, which helped to contribute to his income. He was loyal to the job.

Every village in the South had some type of gatekeeper, who took care of the community and strengthened the families. The gatekeepers made the decisions in the village. They had visions that were attainable, which helped to develop structure in the village. Therefore, exchange of favors- sugar, vegetables, & transportation helped stabilize the village's resources for everyone.

There were very few fights or disagreements about who was in charge in the village, and there was no voting or meetings to choose a gatekeeper in the village. The people had confidence in the gatekeeper, and families were stabilized, thereby, stabilizing the village. It was known through the years that a gatekeeper played a crucial role in building the village; no matter what happened in the village- bridges collapsing, flooding, & crop failure, the gatekeeper found ways to solve the problems.

The gatekeeper learned, firsthand, what was needed in the village. This was especially so because he had personal relationships with neighbors within the village. The gatekeepers found ways to empower the village's economic development directly or indirectly. It thrived in resources, not because of wealth or riches, but because it did not misuse its reservoirs of resources vicariously. Although the

resources were scarce at times, they still survived. The gatekeepers dealt with the environment, to

12

include roads, farms, basic infrastructure, as well as the death of loved ones in the village. On many occasions, they had to toll the bell, which signified death in the village.

The village was a community that was committed to one another. It was a place where values were taught, respected, and embraced. There was little jealousy in the village, and everybody's role was important, especially the children. The people in the village inspired children to attain their goals in the midst of obstacles and, at all times, to accomplish their dreams. However, if the children were disobedient, they were punished.

If one child had an opportunity to attended college, it was a milestone for the whole village, and it helped in providing the resources for them. The village found ways to provide needed resources when necessary.

For example: A young lady attended the local school and developed a skill in playing basketball. She was very sharp in basketball and made an impact at school, which resulted in her going to college and then playing professional basketball in a foreign country. However, she needed help in achieving her goal of college. The village supported her goal by providing clothing, finances, and other valuable resources.

The villagers always encouraged their children to accomplish their dreams with integrity. The people in the village made personal vows to invest in their children's future.

The village was made up of people who were ambitious. What began small, eventually grew into larger communities as the people worked hard together. They began to grow into larger communities. These were communities, which celebrated life, in spite of its challenges. Moreover, they met trouble head on and maintained control over their circumstances. They took pride in their neighborhood, worked together, and got to know one another. Everybody was family. It was a solid foundation anchored in God; a core faith which sustained them. The village helped to improve the lives of the people, and for this reason, they assumed the roles as gatekeepers. The gatekeepers were bound by a commitment to a call.

For example: Hudson Taylor's mission moved him outside his comfort zone to a foreign country. He was extremely determined to fulfill his mission, while struggling with personal tragedies. He focused so much attention on the mission and became less concerned about his impending death. To help solidify his mission, it required a commitment of an entire village and God's guidance.

Gatekeepers had to renew a sense of harmony to enhance sufficient strength in the village. They were genuinely concerned about their neighbor, not expecting any reward in return. They also envisioned a solid foundation for a neighbor to improve their lives during hard times. They held the perspective of Jesus' parable of the Good Samaritan, hoping to engender neighborliness and to achieve a desirable end. The old village's foundation had an infrastructure that was solid and committed. The gatekeepers lived in each community and built a village of integrity. However, as time passed, most of the true gatekeepers died, the caregivers got old, and the village began to self-destruct.

As it was in the past, so it is currently. Gatekeepers are just as important now as they were after the emancipation. While gatekeepers are not as visible as they were in the past, they still exist. Earlier on, we established gatekeepers as those individuals who have worked hand in hand to keep family units strong and who were visible in the communities wherein they lived. As I navigate through this topic, I hope you take away how important the gatekeeper was in the past and how much more important and needed they are now.

The New Village

Today, African Americans reflect on their ancestor's tenacity and challenges for a family unit. However, migration from the south to the north, in search for a better life, divided the village system. Many families were fleeing from the South to find work in large cities, moving to cities like Chicago, Detroit, New Jersey, Los Angeles, New York, and to Canada. The unified family became imbalanced, and the village lost its support system. The plight of the family was however, filled with hopes for a new future with an economic security. Nevertheless, their family livelihood was threatened by a lack of care for their children. Many were forced to send children back to the old, slowly shrinking village. Grandparents bridged the gap between full-time working parents and children in need of care and guidance. They were available for their grandchildren during the transition from farm life to the industrialized factory work. The children went south for the summer, and their grandparents would continue to instill, in them, generational norms and values. The children spent extended periods of times with their grandparents so as not to be left alone.

For a while, this system worked well; money, gas, food, and families progressed. Families purchased homes and cars, and they enjoyed the good life. The second-generation families felt secure knowing that they had back up from an older, trusted generation.

As grandparents grew old, they worked on the farms progressively less because of poor health. Those that moved north with their children were now becoming less able to help. They now needed the help they once provided. They had fewer resources to help to take care of their grandchildren. If grandpa or grandma died, the other would serve as a surrogate for the family; however, when they both were gone, they had no help. This forced families who moved from the country to larger cities to find other alternatives of care for their children

15

while they worked.

At first, life was simple; children were raised absent of negative influences, they were well-mannered, respectful to their parents, and received instructions well. The children listened to their parents' teachings and adapted to their values. However, little by little, as children ventured out, changing aspects of a community, which lacked family values, started to inspire them. The roots of the true village died, and a new village was being formed. We then began to see that new ideology take shape.

Some problems in the new village were derived from lack of education, poverty, and oppression. If social poverty was the only foundation they had in the new village, no insight to an upward mobility seemed possible. The visions were unclear because there was nothing to see. Young children had to literally open their eyes to see further than their contextual environment; their visions in life had been altered by behaviors that were self-destructive. They were held in bondage by the limited vision that existed, which in the past, might have been provided by the village.

The current village that was consistently favorable to life victories has been transformed into more of an oppressor. The ongoing chaos and troubles produced a tragic story of uncertainties and hopelessness. The daughters had full responsibility of the children without a mate and without any help. They had to bear the load alone, and this put an extra strain on the family. Some boys began to get in trouble and became a product of the court system. Girls and boys, over time, began to drop out of school, starting families of their own as single parents, having one or two children. While still remaining in the homes with their parents, new additions to the family stretched the budget to the max.

Issues at a personal level became a pressing problem in the new village. Some people cared less about life and less about their future. Illegal products were being sold. Selling food stamps and drugs-for temporary income became a means of surviving for them. Social growth was stunted due to lack of knowledge as learning was distorted by a false ideology of success.

Social relationships were dominated by a system that caused erosion of the values of the old village. Children were introduced to drugs, killing, stealing, robbing, which became the pathways for economic advancement. People were now seen as figures of power that were driving fancy cars. Having wealth in the new village was based on material gains; sneakers, rims, cars. The new village embodied a new order; it was an order that was against order. Some people from the younger generation were thrust into a lifestyle that effectively destroyed their future.

These problems still exist in the 'modern village', and our children are suffering. Human suffering is difficult to explain when it becomes a norm in society because struggle is viewed as a personal problem; it holds no deep meaning and people are left destitute. Their lifestyle is announced to the world and is ridiculed by many. Their lack of resources, lack of education, and lack of finances all make it difficult to change lifestyles. Furthermore, their current struggles are magnified by technologies that expose their limitations and living conditions.

There are so many misconceptions about personal contribution that must be clarified. We have little idea about how to serve the people. We attempt to serve, but our inherent intellect turns our feelings of compassion into a predictable cynicism about how unlikely it is to get the child outside the norms of the modern village. It requires strength to push people to challenge their circumstances, to change their perspectives, and to celebrate their stability.

Early on, we established gatekeepers as those who worked hand in hand to keep family units strong, and they were visible in the community in which they lived. Their driving values do not affirm the person who is doing the serving. It is essential for those who are serving to interact with these driving values as guiding principles. Therefore, our search for that firm hand in the new village is found within the gatekeeper and the caregiver. The gatekeeper and the caregiver reaffirm a need for cultivation of teaching which influences family life in the new village.

A gatekeeper's expectations for helping people should be realistic but should never deem any situation as totally hopeless. When addressing problems, they must not use a broad-brush approach. Because some people in the new village are downtrodden, their images need to be redefined; they must recognize there are other alternatives that provide a precise method. They must continue to be the salt and the light for people in the village. They have to maintain an attitude of a servant hood to affirm their role. It is not a mission for those who are faint at heart or for those who do not engage the heart. It is not an easy job, but it is very rewarding. Some people will have crises that are common, that may stem from their lack of assets due to poverty. Some problems will be difficult to talk about, and some are private and rarely discussed. A gatekeeper's vision must be to engage, empower, and encourage people to find their path.

What is a vision? Vision is defined as "the ability or instance of great perception, especially of future development." Therefore, the vision of a gatekeeper is very important. It is like the vision of a painter painting a rose. The rose may be too dark and need a lighter shade of red. The painter had to envision the qualities of colors needed to accomplish that vision. Thereby, gatekeepers need to have a general idea or vision that creates, influences, and demonstrates social worth in the new village. They need to stay in touch with the new village so they can move past their negative circumstances.

To enhance the vision, gatekeepers had to have an eye for details just like a painter. The gatekeepers must closely evaluate the people's needs and attend to them individually. Vision to some people is a derivative of faith and a manifestation of things coming to life. Painters envision a picture in the realm of their minds and hearts. Each stroke is taken with precise caution. They paint a picture with a vision that constitutes a reality unfolding-a rose, a landscape.

So, the entrusted gatekeepers have to work based on truth that is revealed through stifling limitations; they must not refrain from their work due to a timeframe, but they must be diligent to an endless process. Ultimately, it could yield the finished work of a masterpiece.

Stabilizing imbalances in the village may take years. Because some people in the village have little control over their circumstances, they are afraid to express their fears. A gatekeeper must continue to work with one person at a time, in pursuit of an ultimate outcome. It has to be an outcome that provides structure for a better lifestyle.

Gatekeepers will be working in a community that has no boundaries in crises. They must not lose their focus based on surrounding circumstances. They have to engage in struggles with the people and help them to face reality. They have to adjust day by day to social circumstances and not be surprised when a crisis occurs. They will encounter circumstances that are sometimes critical, pressing, and stressful. They have to address these crises head on and not be afraid of taking a risk for an ultimate goal.

For example, if the village is experiencing some crises, the gatekeeper has to comfort the community as a whole and encourage them. The discourse in the village challenges gatekeepers. There is a loss of life, people are incarcerated, and people are afraid. Although a group of people is seeking help, the gatekeeper cannot help them all simultaneously. As soon as they attend to the problems affecting the entire village, they must begin to make plans to help the villagers individually. It is imperative to get each of them stabilized, which is the primary focus.

A gatekeeper's role is sometimes overwhelming, and they must be attuned to their own strengths and weaknesses. They must be willing to serve others and design a plan that forms a lasting relationship; a relationship that is desirable, meaningful, and transforming. Relationships have to be intentional but not too intense. The significance of a relationship is to compel them to search for ways out and seek new opportunities.

In 1949, government housing was beginning to take hold in the United States in response to a great concern for new public housing developments. It was such a concern that by 1968, a new housing act was approved, and 2,870 units were built. Fannie Mae introduced section eight housing, and as subsidized housing grew, poor families grew in numbers.

This is a danger for a generation of people. There are external and internal implications that needed to be acknowledged. We must engage the hearts of people. In light of these factors, we walk into the village knowing the ongoing problems of the people. We must have a genuine desire to serve.

19

Subsidized housing was made available for the purpose of helping the poor. It was especially designed to help poor families, elderly, and single women with children. At first, the families that moved in took great pride in taking care of the property. The village concept was still evident. Families knew each other and enjoyed their newfound freedom of space and the joy of having neighbors. Sadly, this freedom was short lived. Within a few years, those properties began to deteriorate, and there arose a crisis in the village. The flower gardens were trampled, broken down cars were parked in yards, and over time, the houses that flourished with life became abandoned and boarded up. For those that were left, an increase of rodents and drugs challenged the mere existence of families living under these conditions. People were sick mentally, physically, and spiritually. The caregivers that were once evident had retreated and no longer took care of their spaces in the village.

For example: The subsidized housing projects such as Cabrini Green in Chicago, Hurt's Village in Memphis, and Brewster Apartment Complex in Detroit became gang infested and unproductive. Human suffering was present in the community. While there was an attempt by churches and welfare organizations to guide people to help, many were going without what they needed to survive from day to day. There seemed to be no escape from this type of living. By 1995, public housing had reached its peak of a downward spiral. There seemed to be very little hope for the village, thus endangering another generation of people to spend their lives in poverty. Nevertheless, many were being helped; however, due to the seriousness of the problems and the number of people who needed help, it seemed only a few were being served. Serving these families on a daily basis helped to curve some disturbances in the community and that, in turn, allowed some young people to thrive. By 2009, many of the subsidized housing complexes had been torn down, forcing families to look for housing elsewhere. Again, we began to see the same problems now existing in subsidized single-dwelling homes.

The language of the gatekeeper has become confused because "papa" and "mama" no longer exist in the newfound communities as they did in the beginning of the old village. Therefore, the community now begins to suffer because it has no true leader. While the gatekeepers still exist in some communities, they have had to retreat and become quiet in response to the overpowering number of ills that continues to manifest itself. Meanwhile, for the most part, the village is running itself and making its own decisions based on immediate gratification, fast money, and illegal trafficking.

The village now gets its information from underground sources that taint its true value. These sources are not fully trustworthy; however, there is a small stream of information that comes from the village that is trustworthy, to which people pay little attention. This trusted information are those elderly people who have been in the community for years and small churches that have been left behind because larger churches branched out into other areas. Those left behind became the remnant to carry on. Others, such as the old corner stores, beauty shops, and barbershops, are still trusted sources. Therefore, communities need to lean heavily on churches and non-profits that have been in the community for years. There are other places that have been in the neighborhood for many years that are reliable gatekeepers as well. The gatekeepers who protected, cared about, created visions, and created confidence in families in the old village are few and hidden.

Despite the obscurity of these sources, they still maintain the same values as the gatekeepers had in the old true village. They remained obscured because of the dangers that exist in the new village. Exposing theses individuals is a sure way of hindering the help they can provide. Obscured gatekeepers, as well as new gatekeepers, are needed to help offer stability to this chaotic environment, which has been created by the new village.

Now we have to look at the new village and how it can be reconstructed to bring hope to a community that is spiraling out of control due to a loss of gatekeepers. So what can one do? Older gatekeepers can have a voice in the community through social media, such as YouTube, or by using recorded information that will last a lifetime. Therefore, letting the elderly tell their stories on camera will preserve their messages. By doing so, their voices will be continually heard by those who want to learn by listening to what they have to say. All is not lost. There are hundreds of children and adults who are seeking information from older, more experienced adults and can incorporate these messages into their daily lives. While it is a revelatory aspect of socialization, it can also be a great tool for establishing a village. Social media brings worlds together by a virtual model of communication. It creates an audience one could only dream about in years past.

There is a need for experienced voices to be continually heard in our neighborhoods. Social media represents a new method for gathering and disseminating information, which is an improvement to the old ways of communicating. Some of the information that is important in our neighborhood can still come in the form of the voices and messages of old gatekeepers that need to be activated once again. What was needed then is still needed now. New gatekeepers also are needed to keep the community in the right perspective.

Future Gatekeepers

In the last few years, there have been some emerging leaders in communities who are not afraid to be there. They are ready to take the responsibility of helping wherever they can. These emerging leaders are to be encouraged and mentored into permanent gatekeepers in communities all over the world. In our conversation, throughout this piece, we have talked about how gatekeepers were known to be present and aware of what was going on in the community. These new leaders must begin to become knowledgeable of the root problem that exists in a neighborhood and work on them one at a time.

The tendency with new leaders is to bite off more than they can chew because they recognize how massive the problems are. By doing this, the ability to help becomes diluted and what they do gets absorbed in the exiting problem. My husband used a phrase that has been important in serving: Stay on your Beam. This means one must grab hold to a rare opportunity and continue to serve in that area until he sees a change. He must do this in spite of seeing a lot of great things going on around him. Staying on the beam will produce results. If you are in an area, you will see college graduates, home owners, business men and women, pastors and community leaders.

Much of what you accomplish will depend on your discipline, sticking with the vision, and staying prayerful and healthy to carry it out. Gatekeepers are recognized for their commitment and 'stickability'. Villages will change and communities will grow as commitments are carried out.

Our Target Group

According to The Urban Child Institute, "The future of our city depends upon how well we mentor our children. Because when it comes to children, what we are looking at is not a money problem, but it is a brain problem. It has been proven by researchers that influences on brain development can be traced back to conception." So, much of the mentoring will have to be done through parents because they are the child's first teacher. Thereby, gatekeepers who are mentors must relay meaningful messages to parents with small children.

In light of what we have learned from these sources, we are convinced that we must reestablish, in every community, strong gatekeepers that take a holistic message to our communities. We must fight back with tools that are available to us. We must retrain and reengage gatekeepers in communities where problems still exist. To do this, we must first begin to identify and partner with as many individuals, churches, and non-profits as possible.

We must also learn everything we can from institutions that are studying the trends in our communities. The scientific evidence is overwhelming: what influences a child's brain development in the earliest years will influence what type of adult he becomes.

So, it is imperative that there is a bond between parent(s) and children, schools and children, and communities and children. We know that old gatekeepers continue to be active in every aspect with children in the old village. Therefore, it is a must that new gatekeepers find innovative ways of bringing wholeness to the new village. Any disconnect or deviation from this concept creates what we see happened with Cabrini Green and other subsidized housing programs.

www.ingramcontent.com/pod-product-compliance
Lightning Source LLC
Chambersburg PA
CBHW051350290326

41933CB00042B/3353